KU-789-051

101 ways to Succeed in Sports Development

Andy Gooding FILAM

Senior Lecturer
Suffolk College

First published: 1998
Second edition: 1999
Third edition: March 2003
ISBN 1 873903 95 2

Institute of Leisure and Amenity Management

Published by

Institute of Leisure and Amenity Management, ILAM House,
Lower Basildon, Reading, RG8 9NE Tel: 01491 874800   Fax: 01491 874801
-mail: info@ilam.co.uk web: www.ilam.co.uk

About the author

Andy Gooding has a first degree in Sport Studies from Newcastle Polytechnic (now University of Northumbria) and an MA in Leisure and Tourism Studies from the University of North London. He has been involved in sports development since 1982, working in the voluntary sector as the manager of the Merseysport project based in Liverpool, in the statutory sector as sports development officer for Trafford MBC in Greater Manchester and in the education sector as the leisure and recreation adviser at Suffolk College in Ipswich. He is a past chair of ILAM Eastern Region and helped to establish the Eastern Region Sports Development Association. He is currently a Running Sport tutor, a member of the Suffolk Sport Committee and was the event organiser of the 2001 Suffolk Youth Games.

Foreword

This guide is aimed at those thinking of entering sports development as a career and at those who have recently taken up a post in sports development for the first time.

It is not intended to be the definitive text on the subject. I have tried to include the sort of things that I wish someone had told me when I first started in sports development. It is written in an informal style and combines relevant background knowledge with practical suggestions about a variety of topics.

Using the framework of '101 ways', I have had to be selective and have chosen topics most likely to be encountered at the beginning of your career in sports development. Hopefully this guide will whet your appetite for the subject and a bibliography is also provided to lead you on to explore these topics in more depth.

Andy Gooding

ILAM and Sports Development

As an institute for leisure professionals from all disciplines, ILAM aims to support individuals' development by offering advice and guidance through a number of sources, including a professional awareness and development programme, professional qualifications, information sheets and journals and of course, publications such as this.

This guide was originally commissioned by the ILAM Sports Services Panel who recognised a need for an easy-to-access, informative document that would provide basic sports development knowledge to newcomers, those thinking of entering sports development, students and old hands alike, remembering that the most experienced of us can always benefit from revisiting the basics of what we do from time to time.

Acknowledgements

This book was originally dedicated to the many people who have helped me to enjoy a career in sports development. I still feel that this is very appropriate. Having been inspired to work in this area by my tutors, Ian Elvin and George Wilkinson, while studying in Newcastle, I have been lucky enough to experience working in Liverpool, the large urban conurbation that dominates Merseyside, in Trafford MBC in the urban fringe of Greater Manchester and in Ipswich, the county town of rural Suffolk. I have been – and still am – very proud to have worked alongside many hundreds of people, both as professional colleagues and people working voluntarily in the sports community, who all have one thing in common: they have a real passion for promoting and developing sport. Keep up the good work!

Particular thanks to colleagues at ILAM House for encouraging the sales of this book, which has sold over 500 copies since it was initially published. It would never have been produced or subsequently updated without their help and support.

Thank you also to Gill, Paul, Julie and Emma Gooding for giving me the space to initially write and then update this book. Yes, it's finished, so let's get back to playing some sport!

Contents

thinking about sports development?

1

Sports development has a high profile. Indeed, it is fair to say that over the last twenty years sports development has become one of the flagships of the leisure industry and, as such, has had a key role to play in changing the culture of organisations involved in the delivery of sports participation and performance.

2

Although many people believe that sports development is a modern idea, looking back through the pages of history it is clear that the concept of sports development came to prominence in the 1930s under the guidance of the Central Council of Physical Recreation and Training (now the CCPR). During the period from the 1930s to 1960s, the CCPRT regional officers were the first to work across local authority boundaries, encouraging a multi-agency, partnership approach in addressing issues such as health-related fitness, sport in school and coach education. In many ways we have come full circle as these issues have once again reached the top of the sports development agenda.

3

The launch of the 'Sport for All' campaign during the 1960s placed sports development securely in the work programme for the new advisory Sports Council. Things were to change in the 1970s. Under the re-organised Sports Councils, with their new executive powers, sports development was generally less prominent in a period that saw much effort concentrated on the rapid expansion in new, purpose-built sports facilities. However, in the early 1980s the Sports Councils were quick to revert to the community sports development approach to address politically sensitive inner-city problems and to extend the sporting franchise to specific target groups through programmes such as Action Sport and the National Demonstration Projects.

4

Although in the late 1980s it seemed likely that sports development would be a casualty of the contract culture with the introduction of compulsory competitive tendering (CCT), it emerged relatively unscathed. Even with the introduction of tighter financial controls, it continued to gain credibility and became even more influential throughout the 1990s, particularly within local authorities and sports governing bodies.

5

In comparison with the 1980s, when there was a rapid growth in the creation of new posts in sports development, the 1990s was a period of consolidation. Sports development had reached a more mature stage in its life cycle with relatively few new posts being created and some being lost. Year on year, although there are a relatively large number of sports development posts advertised, often on a national basis, many are now refilling established positions rather than recruiting for newly created ones. The exception to this rule, as we enter the new millennium, is the growth in new posts associated with the 'Active' programmes (Active Sports, Active Schools and Active Communities) initiated by Sport England with substantial National Lottery funding.

(see Appendix A)

6

So what does 'sports development' actually mean? It is not a particularly easy idea to define. It aims to make a difference to the provision of sport at all levels by challenging traditional attitudes and beliefs and by encouraging positive action to bring about a process of necessary change. It emphasises the importance of the way in which sports opportunities are delivered in the community. It seeks to remove the barriers that hinder sports participation and to make access more universally available, particularly for specific groups known to be under-represented. It also encourages pathways for the development of specific sports from participation through to excellence using specialist coaching groups and school-club links. It promotes opportunities for coach education, training for sports administrators and seeks to co-ordinate action to ensure the best use of limited resources.

7 In order to succeed, sports development must be clear about the way in which sports opportunities should be structured and sure that programmes are focused on clear strategic aims and objectives. The two most useful frameworks for thinking about sports development are the:

(i) **Sports Development Continuum**. This has been around for many years and uses the terms 'foundation', 'participation', 'performance' and 'excellence' to distinguish the transition from learning the basic skills to elite performance.

(ii) **Sports Development Performance Pathway** is the version currently in vogue and uses the terms 'Getting Started', 'Keeping Going', 'Getting Better' and 'Being The Best' to describe the key stages in sports development process.

Such models are particularly useful as they help you to identify the different approaches required to meet the needs of participants as they reach, and move between, the different stages (Appendix B).

8 Over the last sixty years or so, sports development has had an ability to change its image to suit the needs of the time, reflecting key political and social issues and attracting new resources to move the work forward. Without doubt, it has been opportunist in its approach but it has been very influential in justifying investment in sport, both as a means to an end (eg health promotion, economic development and social cohesion) and as a worthwhile activity in its own right.

9 Sports development work is found in many different contexts and access to resources is often limited. Therefore sports development has had to adapt, offering a wide variety of approaches to achieve its aims. 'Generalists' at one end of the spectrum may be expected to work at all levels of the sports development continuum with a wide cross-section of the community. 'Specialists' at the other end may be working to a narrower brief in more depth, concentrating on a specific community group, working within a school or perhaps developing performance and excellence in a particular sport. In between are a wide range of roles and responsibilities under the sports development umbrella.

10 **Why is sports development especially valued?**

- It has been at the leading edge of new initiatives.
- It is a marketing asset and, as such, has the ability to create a positive image for the host organisation.
- It has a direct community focus with staff often based within the community that they serve.
- It has been centrally involved in the strategic planning of leisure services.
- It has encouraged new investment in leisure services even at times when there have been substantial cuts in revenue funding. In particular, it has received substantial grant aid from the Sports Councils.

working environment

11

Sports development has a popular image and, as result, competition for vacant posts is very keen. There are no specific qualifications needed to work in sports development. Some vacancies ask for a general standard of education and an interest in sport. Others ask for more specific sports/leisure-related academic qualifications (eg AVCE, diploma or degree) or other relevant professional qualifications (eg ILAM, ISRM, teaching or youth and community work). The emergence of sports development has provided the opportunity for graduates, usually with leisure and recreation qualifications, to gain direct entry into junior and middle management positions within the leisure industry, by-passing the traditional route, which was to gain promotion by working your way up through the ranks from a sports assistant.

12

Over the years, as more substantial job opportunities have been created, a career structure within sports development has begun to emerge. In general terms, entry into sports development work is possible at three levels: sports leader, sports development officer and sports development manager. Although appointments with a clear sports development brief have been created up to assistant director level, it is generally the case that progression into more senior management posts requires a broader, more general leisure management perspective, of which sports development is but one aspect.

13

For sports leaders, the work usually involves promoting, organising and running sessions which brings you into direct contact with participants. Sports governing body coaching awards and/or community sports leadership qualifications and a first aid certificate are essential prerequisites. As a sports development officer or manager, the work is less hands-on and more resource-based. The more senior the sports development post, the more necessary it is that candidates can demonstrate to potential employers something more than practical sports leadership or coaching skills. Supervision of staff, strategic planning, time management, marketing and financial management are more relevant at this level. Equally, knowledge of equal opportunities, health and safety, child protection and quality assurance are also very important. It is essential to keep up to date with current policies and programmes of the national sports organisations and have a good insight into policy areas, such as the National Curriculum, and sources of funding, such as the National Lottery.

14

Whether you are working as part of a dedicated sports development team or as a lone sports development officer, it is likely that for part, or all, of your work you will be expected to manage your own programme. As such, at times, you may feel somewhat isolated. For many people, the opportunity to rely on their own judgement, initiative and expertise is what makes working in sports development rewarding, although it also means that you must be self-motivated and you carry a weight of responsibility that should not be dismissed lightly.

15

When you arrive, all eyes will be on you and you will need to make a good impression from the start. Expectations will be high and pressure will be on you to deliver results. You need to be firm and agree from the outset a period of at least three months to give you time to plan your work before you attempt to take action. Clear objectives and a well thought out work programme are the basic framework for a successful sports development programme. Ad hoc progress may bring short-term success but it will inevitably result in long-term problems.

16 Many sports development posts are still offered on short-term contracts (average 2-3 years). This puts added pressure on the person appointed, as the long-term future of the post is uncertain. Given that it is good practice to use the initial period (6-8 months) to plan the programme, this leaves relatively little time to show what can be achieved.

17 You should expect to be given an induction programme, which gives you an insight into the workplace and the external environment in which you will be working. It is important that you get to know your own organisation and its objectives. It is also essential to understand the procedures to which you are expected to conform. Is there an annual cycle with key dates for committee reports, annual reports and financial statements? What are your responsibilities for staff supervision, budgetary control, health and safety, etc? What opportunities are there for your continuing professional development?

18 It is an error to think that because sports development involves outreach work you should work in isolation from the rest of your organisation. Sports development is all too often seen as an optional extra rather than considered as a part of the core service. As many of your colleagues will not really understand the nature of your job, you should make every effort to keep your colleagues informed of what you are doing and what is being achieved. Not just council members and senior management but your colleagues in general.

19 Don't hesitate to make contact with potential partners in the local community. Identify key individuals, not just from the obvious mainstream organisations but others, such as housing action groups and detached youth workers, who may not have a clear sports development brief but who have specialist knowledge that may help you. Explain what your role is and seek their advice and opinions but don't promise more than you can deliver. Some will be enthusiastic to support your work and draw on your expertise to help them achieve their own goals. Others will be sceptical, perhaps because they have had a poor experience from your organisation or your predecessor in the past. Consultation can help others buy into your programme and will help them to better understand your particular role.

20 Make use of existing networks.

- Most districts will have one or more local Sports Councils that will bring you into contact with local clubs, leagues and sports administrators.
- The Health Authority will have health promotion specialists.
- The local Education Authority will have an adviser who can put you in touch with the local schools PE network and the Schools' Sports Association.
- Community education and the youth service can help direct you to a whole range of possible partners including the Duke of Edinburgh's Award Scheme.
- Most counties have sports development forums that will help you to meet other people that share your specialist interest. To work well the forums must be more than 'talkshops'. They can ensure a co-ordinated approach to areas such as coach education programmes, provide help and support for new colleagues and exert collective pressure to lobby for resources or change. Time invested in contributing to such forums should provide payback in the form of advice, joint working and professional development.

21

Because of the entrepreneurial nature of sports development work, you will probably have the opportunity to pursue new and exciting areas of work. However, 'new product development' has a high risk of failure and a planned approach is required to identify worthwhile opportunities. This is particularly important in the first year of your appointment, when making the right decisions and creating a good first impression provides a sound platform on which to progress in the longer term. The right decisions may provide opportunities, which could lead to additional resources and support. Poor decisions may create millstones that are difficult to leave behind as the project develops.

22 As so much sports participation takes place outside normal office time, unsociable hours are an inevitable part of the working environment. This can create a problem because you are rarely in the office and are therefore not 'seen' to be doing your job. It is also a problem to organise adequate space for your own social life, rest and recreation.

23 Inevitably there will be more work than you will be able to cope with effectively. Be realistic about what you can achieve. Take time, in the first place, to review what resources are available, what is already happening and consider what changes are on the horizon that may have an effect on your work.

24 Learn to say 'no'! Quality rather than quantity is important. A limited but achievable programme is better than a wide-ranging, unco-ordinated, ad hoc approach. 'Burn out' is all too common in development work. It is easy to become seriously over-committed because you like to be positive and say 'yes', rather than be considered negative by saying 'no'. Consider each new opportunity in the context of your work programme: does it help to meet your objectives? If not, explain why you cannot help at this time. However, don't be too rigid in your approach. High-impact opportunities in the early days of the project can be useful from a public relations point of view. If circumstances have changed or if there is something that you have missed, revisit your work programme and see if it is possible to make the necessary alterations without altering the overall workload.

sports equity

25 Recognising that there is an inequality of opportunity to take part in sport is one thing but trying to redress the balance is another. The need to remove the barriers that prevent active involvement in sport has been long recognised and much discussed but making headway has not proved easy. As such, sports equity is still the biggest challenge that faces sports development and it should underpin all that you seek to achieve in your development strategy.

26 It would be wrong to say that no progress has been made over the last thirty years. Without doubt, there are many examples of good practice. Encouraged by the Sports Councils, many successful schemes have targeted specific under-represented populations and concentrated on removing the more visible physical, social and economic barriers. However, it is disappointing to think that despite over thirty years of campaigning under the 'Sport for All' banner, inequality in sport still stubbornly persists.

27 Whether sport is socially acceptable as an end in itself (as a basic right) or as a means to another end (eg health benefits, community development, economic regeneration, social integration, personal challenge, etc) is a matter for political debate. What is generally recognised is that people of all backgrounds and abilities have a basic right to play and achieve their personal goals in sport. However, clearly this is still not universally the case.

28

The 1995 Disability Discrimination Act once again placed disability high on the agenda and offers a good starting point for progress in this area. However, physical disability is only one of the many important aspects of sports equity. As such, the Act should not totally deflect your attention from the overall aim of sports equity which is to make sport equally accessible to everyone at all levels of the sports development continuum, including young people, women, people from ethnic minorities and people with learning difficulties. It also involves encouraging the principle of fair play and changing attitudes and perceptions of others involved in sport, including officials, administrators and spectators.

29

Championing the cause of sports equity is not a soft option. In an economic climate with continued financial restraints, sports equity work does not always sit comfortably alongside the need for economic efficiency. Innovative work with under-represented groups is inherently time-consuming and costly with a high risk of failure. It's up to you to fight your corner on such issues to ensure that resources are distributed on an equitable basis and that income generation does not become the sole objective of sports development, diluting its effectiveness.

30

Sports equity should be the keystone for policies within your sports development strategy. Drawing from the strategy, you may wish to publish a specific sports equity statement with measurable objectives that clearly signals your intentions to existing and potential partners. In this way, through the cascade effect, you will help to ensure that the principles of sports equity are put into practice. In a similar way, it should be possible to raise awareness of sports equity issues and provide the incentive for change at a local level by ensuring that criteria for discretionary rate relief, access to grant aid and support for national lottery bids incorporates the sports equity message.

the marketing mix

31 Marketing is still a 'buzz word' that is commonly used but not well understood. The term 'marketing' is somewhat confusing because it refers both to a way of thinking about quality service delivery, which places the customer at the centre of the operation, and also to various management techniques. These marketing techniques, developed mainly by the commercial sector, help to ensure that what is offered meets an identified need, and in so doing, gives a return on the investment made. Sports development has naturally evolved a marketing orientation because it places the needs of the customer first but in general it fails to see the importance of applying marketing techniques in what is essentially a non-profit environment.

32 Don't be put off! The beauty of marketing is that it offers you a framework and a set of tools that, if used in a planned way, can help you to make sure that your programme has every chance of being successful. All sports development programmes make use of various marketing techniques in the everyday management of their programmes. The problem lies in recognising the right tools to use and in understanding the advantages that marketing planning and control offers over the ad hoc approach.

33 The basic idea behind marketing is that it helps to reduce uncertainty about whether people will use the services that you offer, regardless of whether or not this involves making a profit. It is worth remembering that leisure activities are a perishable commodity and funding of services is discretionary. If the services are not used, they cannot be stored away for another time. As such, they are lost and, if this continues, in time questions will inevitably be asked about the need for such provision (ie the balance between the cost of providing the service you offer against other service opportunities that are lost through lack of available funding).

34 Because you are: working at arms length through volunteers, sports leaders and facility managers; in partnership with different organisations and agencies; having to rely on political will; seeking good publicity; raising the funds, etc, you need to have a clear idea of what you are trying to achieve. Committing this to paper is easier said than done.

35 This is where a marketing plan, as part of your overall sports development strategy, can help. It can focus your thoughts on:

- what you are trying to achieve (marketing objectives)
- the information you need to have at your disposal (marketing research)
- who are you aiming your services at
- the best marketing tools to use (marketing mix)
- the resources available
- the time-scale required
- how you will gain feedback on the success of the programmes (quality control)
- how you will react if things do not go according to plan (contingency measures)

36 Awareness of current polices and consultation with colleagues and the community will play a part in deciding the appropriate marketing mix for your programme. In particular it will help in deciding upon the:

- product policy (eg which services to offer, focus sports to adopt, coach education sessions to run)
- pricing options (eg the cost of an activity session, a training course or the

use of concessionary passes)

- distribution of the services (eg the selection of the venues, partners involved, timing, etc)

- communications mix (ie getting your message across to the right audience whether it involves making a presentation to the local Sports Council, producing a sports directory, generating media coverage, offering taster sessions or negotiating a sponsorship deal)

37 Marketing is not something to be left to a central marketing unit or designated marketing manager. Most of your programme decisions will have marketing implications. As such, you have an important stake in the marketing effort. Although many important decisions are not under your control, those that are can be effectively used to help influence the decision-making process in your favour.

38 Without doubt your work would be much easier if you had more control over what was going on in the external environment. The environment in which you work is constantly changing and by the very nature of your work you are repackaging activities and testing new ideas for participants who are recognised as non-users of the services already available. To reduce the level of uncertainty to an acceptable level and increase the chances of success, you need to manage the resources under your control to their best advantage by using the marketing tools at your disposal.

39 Marketing a service has added problems in that the product cannot be fully produced in advance because the customer plays a key part in the production process. While you can provide the facilities, staffing and equipment, it is the actual use by the participants that completes the delivery of the service. Even with the payment of a fee, the customer does not take ownership of anything and leaves only with an impression of the service offered. It is therefore essential that the quality of the experience matches or exceeds their expectations every time.

40 However, a high quality of service delivery is inherently difficult to maintain, as it is the interaction of the participants among themselves and with the staff that will determine whether the participants enjoy their experience and return next time. This relies on awareness of the need for good customer care. In this respect, it is important to ensure that you build strong customer loyalty based on a good 'word of mouth' reputation and a strong brand image.

raising sponsorship

41 Sponsorship is a business arrangement from which both parties should gain some advantage. It should not be seen as a charitable gift and is not the answer to all your problems! Its value can be judged in terms of the marketing benefits it offers to you and the return on investment it offers to the sponsor, compared with similar expenditure on other forms of communication such as advertising, sales promotion and exhibition stands.

42 ### Gaining sponsorship is very competitive

Requests far outweigh the resources available and it is important that your proposal stands out from the rest. As in many other areas, first impressions count.

43 Show that you mean business and prepare a sponsorship pack that outlines whom you represent, what you wish their organisation to sponsor, the time-scale involved and what marketing opportunities you can offer in return. If you have worked with other sponsors, show what you have achieved through this relationship. Include press cuttings that credit previous sponsors to show that you have good media contacts. Above all, give a professional image.

44

To find a sponsor, do some research. Build up a list of possible contacts. Look to local sponsors for local initiatives and to national sponsors for opportunities that have a national profile. Make use of existing networks such as the Chamber of Commerce, Rotary Club or Round Table. Also consider your own suppliers, ask colleagues for suggestions and look to see who is actively marketing their products in your area.

45

Once you have established a suitable contact list, try to find out more about each of the organisations and, in particular, identify the name of the individual within the company who has a responsibility for sponsorship. Obtain their annual report; enquire if they have a sponsorship policy; find out when their financial year begins. By being knowledgeable about the organisation and their marketing activities, you can tailor your offer to meet their needs and, in this way, enable them to reach a considered decision.

46

Mail out all your packs with a suitable covering letter but don't hold your breath waiting for a reply! In most cases, you will need to follow up your letter with a phone call a couple of weeks later. Be persistent but don't burn your bridges, as you may wish to go back another time. If you get a negative reply, ring to find out why and ask whether they would consider an opportunity for sponsorship in the future. The more feedback you get, the more effective you will be in forming your offer next time.

47 Remember that getting a response to the sponsorship pack is only the first step. Should you receive a positive reply, you will then need to discuss what they have in mind and consider how this fits in with your plans. Is sole sponsorship the only option or could you do more using a multi-sponsor approach? How does the sponsor require their name/logo and corporate colours to be used in the promotional material? How and by when will the sponsorship monies be paid? If they don't suit what you have in mind, say so.

48 If possible, arrange to meet with the sponsors in person. In this way you will be able to judge with whom you are dealing and will be able to get a feel for the organisation, and the people, with whom you will be working. You may be asked to deal with the organisation direct or through their marketing/advertising agency. Agencies in particular will be experienced in negotiating sponsorship deals and will look to gain maximum value for money. Be flexible and creative in meeting their needs but don't promise what you can't deliver or agree to something, such as hospitality for the sponsor's guests, that may end up costing you more than the sponsorship is worth. Equally, don't be afraid to seek their advice and use their expertise as part of the sponsor arrangement. They may have some useful contacts or access to celebrities that could improve still further your chances of success.

49 Once you have agreed the terms of the sponsorship, get it confirmed in writing to avoid any misunderstandings. If they don't write to you, you should write to them confirming these details and you can raise any issues that need to be clarified.

50 As you move on with the project, keep the sponsors or their agents informed of your

progress. If there are appropriate occasions, invite them to attend and send copies of press releases and press-cuttings that include reference to them. In this way you are more likely to build up a longer-term relationship.

51

What if things go wrong? Honesty is an essential ingredient in all

successful sponsorship agreements. Even if things do not go entirely to plan, always keep your sponsors informed. In this way you will keep their door open should the opportunity for sponsorship arise again in the future.

developing partnerships

52

The restructuring of local authority leisure service departments, initially in response to compulsory competitive tendering (CCT) and the continued restriction in the availability of capital and revenue funding, has moved many local authorities away from direct delivery of services towards an enabling role. This has opened up greater opportunities for working in partnership with both the voluntary and commercial sectors.

53

Partnership can have both a positive and a negative influence on sports development programmes. If the benefits accrue to all the partners involved then the combined effect can deliver more than any of the partners could do working on their own. However, the opposite can also happen if the partners are poorly matched and the effect is one of frustration and lost opportunity.

54

Partnerships involve two or more parties in the pursuit of mutually agreed and identified objectives. They can simply involve the intention to co-operate in certain areas of mutual interest or they can result in a more formal, contractual obligation with a specific purpose in mind. They may take the form of an equal partnership with each organisation contributing resources, in cash or in kind, and with each benefiting equally from the success of the programme. Alternatively, the partnership may result in a 'lead body' taking on all the operational aspects with approval and/or financial support from the other 'silent' partners. The nature of the agreement will determine whether or not a formal working group is required to overview the operational aspects of the partnership.

55

The more extensive the partnership, the more complicated it is to manage effectively. The culture of the different organisations involved in the partnership may mean that the pace of progress proves to be slower than was expected, particularly where it is likely to cross boundaries and levels of authority within and between organisations. Some people may have delegated decision-making authority and others may have to refer every decision back to their senior managers or committees. Each partner will have to justify their involvement in the partnership by demonstrating that it is a cost-effective method of achieving their objectives. In trying to meet everyone's objectives, the original purpose of the partnership can get lost.

56

Communication is an essential feature in any partnership.
It is important that all partners are kept well informed of progress made and, appropriate to their role in the group, are able to influence the decision-making process. However keen and enthusiastic members of the partnership may be, at some stage it is likely that areas of potential conflict will arise. If problems are not addressed openly and attempts made to resolve them

satisfactorily for all concerned, the credibility of the partnership will be lost. This may have a wider and/or longer lasting effect, jeopardising more than just the present arrangements.

57

The level of skill required to negotiate and influence others in nurturing partnerships should not be underestimated. As a sports development specialist, you will often be the person who brings the partners together and it is essential that you judge whether it is necessary to offer your continued involvement to make the partnership work. You need to consider how sustainable your involvement will be in the life of the partnership. Be open about your intentions from the beginning; successful partnerships are based on mutual trust and honesty.

58

Always give credit where credit is due, as this helps to build a longer-term relationship that may result in future joint initiatives. Whilst it is important, for all sorts of reasons, for you to make your work known, it is not always necessary to be seen to be taking the leading role. Providing support and advice, and encouraging others to succeed in taking the initiative forward, can result in a more credible word of mouth reputation and enable your earlier withdrawal, if appropriate. It is also vital to respect the input of all involved, whether theirs is a professional or voluntary contribution.

time management

59

Working in sports development you will soon be aware that time is one of your most valuable resources and one that has to be consciously managed to ensure that it is used effectively. Better use of time can help you to be more productive, feel less stressed and more in control of what you are doing.

60 Allow yourself time to think! Time is a relative concept: it can seem to pass too quickly (eg deadlines that catch up with before you are ready) or too slowly (eg waiting for the result of an application for grant aid from the National Lottery). The old BT advertising slogan 'work smarter, not harder' is worth remembering. Working 'smarter' includes giving yourself time to think about what you are doing, analysing where your time goes and trying out simple ideas that really can help you to improve your performance.

61 Don't continually put yourself under pressure by not thinking ahead. Be realistic and allow yourself sufficient time to complete tasks. Make sure when agreeing a deadline that you build in a reasonable contingency for unexpected delays. When you are waiting for key decisions to be made, put them out of your mind and concentrate on the things that you can actually influence.

62 You may like to think that having a flexible approach to your work schedule and having an open door policy are qualities that set you apart from your colleagues but look more carefully at how you use your time. Try keeping a time diary, noting how you make use of your work and social time. It may surprise you to find how poorly you manage your time when you calculate how much time is wasted by unnecessary tasks, by other people interrupting you and through being disorganised. By planning and prioritising your work, your life will be less pressurised and more enjoyable.

63 It may not seem like it but time management is a skill that can be consciously improved. There are many good books and short courses on the subject. They all offer sound advice and you will know it makes sense but the problem may be that it does not seem to work for you in practice. In recognising the need for improving your time management, you have taken the first important step. The second step is to find out what techniques suit your personality and will fit your daily routine. Try different ones out. Once you have found one you feel comfortable with, stick with it and allow yourself time to think and evaluate your progress. Each small step can make a difference.

64 Telephones can be time savers but also time wasters if not properly managed. If you have administrative support, arrange to filter the incoming calls to establish whether the enquiry actually needs your attention or, perhaps, could be more easily dealt with by someone else. It is surprising how often sports development automatically gets the non-routine enquiries because no one else bothers to think about where the enquiry really needs to be placed.

65 It is likely that you will be away from your administrative base much of the time. For people trying to reach you, this can become frustrating. Clear communication about your movements and availability to receive calls will help make the system work better. A mobile phone or paging service, an answerphone, a fax machine and e-mail facilities will enable other people to communicate with you without having to waste their time by trying over and over again. Learn how to use the various functions including diverting calls and the redial features. Make a point of regularly checking what messages have been left for you and decide in what order of priority they will be dealt with. If you are going to be out of the office for more than a day, change the message on the answerphone to let the callers know and leave a number where you can be reached, if they need to contact you urgently.

66

Make best use of the technology available. It is often
under-utilised because we don't really understand how to use it or to maximise its full potential. It always pays to read the instruction manuals first. It is surprising how many of us give a cursory glance at the instructions and then dive straight in! Ideally, go on a course and learn how to get the best from the facilities available. There are short courses for beginners and those with more advanced skills on using e-mail, databases, desk-top publishing and website design. However, if you already make use of e-mails and a fax, don't be tempted into constantly using them to bail you out of an emergency situation because you have left something to the last minute!

67

Meetings seem to be an inevitable part of sports development and can easily take control of your schedule, eating away large chunks of your valuable time. **You will be asked to attend a wide range of meetings and should always ask yourself if the benefits of the meetings you attend justify the investment of your time.** Is it necessary that you attend them all? If keeping informed is the main aim, could the same results be achieved by telephone, e-mail or by receiving the minutes of the meetings through the post? If you do need to attend in person, make sure that you are well prepared.

68

If the meeting is not well organised or not properly structured, be prepared to raise the issue with the members present. Other people may be thinking the same things as you but have not had the courage to say so. Be constructive. Clarify with those present the purpose of the meeting and ask how successful they think the meeting has been in achieving it. Encourage suggestions about ways in which the meeting can be improved next time.

69

If you are chairing a meeting, it is important to let people know what the meeting is about and how they should prepare for it. In this respect, sending the agenda or briefing notes out in good time is crucial. Setting the agenda is a skill in itself. Don't make the agenda too long. Only include what it is necessary to discuss and indicate who is speaking to each item and how much time has been allowed. Place the most important issues at the top of agenda so that they are not hurried at the end of the meeting. Don't waste time reading and approving the previous minutes unless it is essential and only allow any other business if it has been notified beforehand.

what a performance!

70

Long gone are the days when, within the public leisure services and the voluntary sector, it was sufficient to justify the expenditure of public funds on leisure provision under broad social and economic objectives. Challenged by the Audit Commission, all providers of leisure services are continually having to justify the level of funding they receive by measuring performance against set objectives and in this way demonstrate that best value has been obtained from the resources used. Sports development is no exception.

71

The introduction by central government of a duty of best value on local authorities has had a subtle but significant impact on sports development.

However hard-working and committed you, your staff and volunteers are, your efforts will be considered of limited use if you have no clear direction and guidelines to measure your performance against. It is as well to be aware that measuring and evaluating performance (the relationship between input, output and outcomes) has become the 'litmus test' for your work and as such, you need to be well informed about this aspect of management control.

72

Monitoring and evaluation is a continuous, on-going activity that enables those responsible for managing resources to determine whether or not their programme is moving in the right direction and is achieving what is intended. It is all too easy for the resources at your disposal to be invested in maintaining programmes that have long since achieved their objectives or to continue to provide taster events or leadership training without considering what is the next step for participants.

73

Self-assessment is an important part of the best value approach but your evaluation must be based on more than subjective assumptions about the worth of the programme. Although there are strong arguments against an over-reliance on quantitative measures because of the qualitative nature of sports development work, it is important to use objective measures that can provide evidence that clearly demonstrates to other people outside the team that your work is meeting identified needs and represents best value. Clearly a balanced view of the quantitative and qualitative aspects of the work is essential in determining what measures are used so that they do not lead to a decrease in responsiveness, quality and innovation.

74

The ethos of best value will expect that your work arises out of a written policy for the provision of leisure services in your area. Your sports development plan must be based on clearly defined objectives and standards of performance. These need to be agreed in advance and must be measurable. The 3 Es (economy, efficiency and effectiveness), plus quality, provide a useful framework.

75 The 'economy' indicators can be covered by a statement of accounts that indicate the actual amount spent and the income generated by a sports development programme. This gives a useful overview of financial control and accountability and can be used to show unit costs. It also allows comparison with expenditure in other areas. However, economy indicators are only one of the performance indicators that should be used to judge performance, as they give no clue as to whether the expenditure itself is justified.

76 As part of your monitoring, you may need to be able to demonstrate the 'efficiency' of your programme by comparing the output against the investment made in it. This view of performance involves the use of financial ratios that have become increasingly popular since compulsory competitive tendering (CCT) was first introduced, as they allow different programmes to be compared using standard formats. There are far more of these ratios than you will need to use and it is important to select the ones most relevant for your programme.

77 The 'effectiveness' of a sports development programme is one of the most difficult aspects to justify and, as a result, tends to get ignored. To consider effectiveness it is necessary to review the performance of your programmes against the objectives set. It is also important to take into account an overview of customer care and quality assurance.

78 To be able to make objective judgements in these areas, consultation is a vital element and should be on-going throughout the process. Ask for regular feedback about your programmes and the services offered. Feedback should not only come from customers but also from front-line staff as they deal directly with the customer and will have a useful contribution to make. Surveys should be planned at regular intervals. The use of written questionnaires can provide information from existing customers, non-users and lapsed users. Telephone surveys and focus groups are also useful but involve more specialist techniques. Specialist computer software programmes are available, making the production of the questionnaires and the subsequent data analysis less time-consuming. Links with your local college or university may also prove beneficial in this respect.

79

From the information collected, you can provide an analysis of the findings and explanation of its relevance, including how it compares with previous periods and recommendations for future action. Depending on the structure of your programme and the partners involved, you may decide to provide quarterly progress reports as well as an annual report. Good communication with your stakeholders is a vital and these reports need to be well presented. They should provide the reader with clear evidence of the progress made against the targets set, based on details of the monitoring and evaluation that has been undertaken during the period under review.

80

Whatever approach you take to the monitoring and evaluation of your sports development work, it is important to bear in mind that the collection of information is not an end in itself; it is ultimately a means of helping you make decisions about the future direction of the programme.

To save time, wasted effort and unnecessary stress, it is essential that the process for the collection of evidence is built into the programme from the start. **It is far more difficult and time-consuming to retrace your steps looking for the evidence at the end of each year. In your haste, good evidence will inevitably be missed or forgotten.**

voluntary effort

81

Stop to think and you will find that in many of the organisations that you deal with volunteers are an essential element at all levels, contributing their time freely for the love of their sport. It is estimated by the UK Sports Council that there are in excess of 1.5 million volunteers making a contribution to sport, which, if costed out, would be worth approximately £1.5 billion each year.

82

The importance of voluntary sports clubs and associations in the development of sports participation, performance and excellence far outweighs the contributions made by any other sector. As such, voluntary effort is a vital element in the sports development process and your professional expertise should be readily available as a resource that can be used by volunteers to help them to continue to carry out their work even more effectively.

83

Voluntary does not simply mean unpaid. It also refers to the fact that the services offered don't have to be provided; they are non-statutory; and offered by choice. Many voluntary organisations have paid staff and, although it is likely that you will have more direct contact with them because of their daytime availability, the contribution of their colleagues, who freely volunteer their services, should not be underestimated nor undervalued. Equally, voluntary effort should not be equated with amateurism. The majority of volunteers have professional knowledge and nationally recognised qualifications or expertise in their own field and they may well have had a longer involvement in their chosen sport than you. Their opinions should always be given careful consideration and clarification offered where your views differ from theirs.

84

It is fair to say that most voluntary organisations do not realise the full potential from the voluntary effort available to them. Through the lack of a co-ordinated approach to the recruitment, training and retention of volunteers, much voluntary effort is wasted and too many volunteers suffer 'burn out' from poor management. The warning signs are usually a reluctance to become involved in the tasks they are normally keen to do or poor performance of their routine tasks. Other signs include late arrival and leaving early, negative rather than positive comments about the organisation or just not appearing to be their usual self.

85

Volunteering is a two way process. The organisation will have its reasons for using voluntary help and all volunteers will have their own personal agenda for volunteering, whether this is explicit or sub-conscious. By freely giving their time and effort, even in doing the most mundane tasks, the volunteer may, in return, be:

• looking to find an opportunity for self-expression, social contact or self-respect.
• seeking to fulfil a sense of civic duty through community service
• seeking to gain an opportunity for personal development or work experience

86

Whatever their reasons, it is essential that volunteers should be able to gain a sense of satisfaction and a sense of achievement from their work because they have been able to make a contribution to clearly defined tasks, had access to the necessary resources to do the job and made to feel part of the team.

87

Before recruiting volunteers, it is worth preparing a job description and a person specification in the same way as you would for a paid worker. This should help you to identify whether there is a clear need for the volunteer(s). The job description should clearly show:

• what tasks are to be undertaken

• what level of responsibility the volunteer will have

• what commitment is required over what period of time

• what training and support is available

The person specification should also indicate what personal qualities and skills are necessary for the volunteer to be able to carry out the work successfully.

88

Some organisations take this a stage further by using volunteer agreements that provide clarification of mutual expectations, obligations and conditions of service. Whether or not you decide that it is appropriate to encourage the use of volunteer agreements, it is important to outline what support is available to the volunteers, including how to claim out-of-pocket expenses. Within the organisation, before recruitment takes place, there is a need to identify who will provide the initial induction training, ongoing supervision, on-the-job training and appraisal of the volunteers. It is important to consider health and safety issues and ensure that adequate insurance cover is provided for voluntary workers.

89 Once in post, good communication with volunteers is important. Make them feel welcome, acknowledge their help and, as far as possible, involve them in making decisions about their work. Regularly review their on-going roles and provide them with opportunities to learn new skills. If appropriate, consider offering progression towards increased responsibility. Also keep a record of each volunteer's experience for future reference.

90 Volunteers are more or less free agents; they are neither protected or constrained by employment contracts. As such, there is less direct control over their actions than for paid staff. However, if problems arise, they must be dealt with accordingly. Ignoring the situation can cause difficulties for your clients, the organisation and other members of staff (both paid and unpaid), as well as for the volunteer. Be positive, be fair and be supportive but remember that you have a service to deliver. Dismissal is an option that you should consider where the situation is unlikely to be resolved by other means.

91 To help you make best use of voluntary help, Sport England, in conjunction with Sports Coach UK, have developed the 'Valuing Volunteers' key course home study pack and workshop as part of the Running Sport programme. It deals with recruiting, retaining and recognising volunteers in sports organisations. Your time would be well spent obtaining the study pack and attending one of these workshops, as they are reasonably priced, well tutored and offer practical solutions to real problems that you may face in working with volunteers.

career progression

92

Sports development is still a relatively new area of the leisure industry and it is worth noting from the outset that there is no clear career structure for progression into senior management posts purely as a specialist in sports development. However, the continued expansion of some sports development programmes has seen the appointment of senior sports development managers in local authorities, in the national Sports Councils and in some of the sports national governing bodies. It is also worth noting that an ever-increasing number of directors and chief executives of leisure organisations have a background in sports development.

93

Generally, progression as a specialist in sports development is limited above middle management. As in many vocational areas, the more senior the management post, the more general the portfolio of responsibility and the more remote the contact with the customers. For many people, the satisfaction of sports development comes from the opportunity of working directly with people in the community. It is why they entered sports development and progression into more senior posts may be considered inappropriate because it would take them away from the source of their job-satisfaction.

94

Whether or not progression is part of your career plan, it is important to continue with your professional development. Learning should be seen as a life-long process. Pay particular attention to the general transferable skills such as communication, working with others, numeracy, information

technology, problem solving and managing tasks.

It is by continually developing these key skills that you will be able to offer an even more professional service. You will also be able to cope more easily with the pace of change in the workplace and generally keep your career options open, giving you the opportunity to progress into senior management posts or to change direction completely, should you so wish.

95 Colleges and universities provide access to leisure-related and general certificates, diplomas and degrees in supervisory, management and business studies, either on a full or part-time basis. Ask for a prospectus and contact their careers/educational guidance advisers for advice on finding the best course to suit your needs. They generally offer the information and interviews free of charge. It is interesting to note that many leisure and recreation qualifications now have a specialist sports development option, or pathway, and for those who seek higher academic qualifications, there are now Masters Degrees in Sports Development.

96 ILAM and other professional Institutes provide a range of qualificatory courses, both college-based and distance learning. They also provide short courses and seminars that are invaluable for updating your knowledge on specific subjects. Contact the appropriate Institute and ask their education and training unit for further information.

97 ## It is not always necessary to have the formal certificated qualifications to meet the prerequisites of a course of study. Increasingly, the accreditation of prior experiential learning – or APL, as it is commonly known – is offered as a means of gaining credit for education and training already gained through voluntary or unpaid work or a previous course that that was left unfinished.

98

Watch out for job opportunities. Scan the local and

national press, join ILAM and receive the weekly job vacancies issued by the appointments service; read the leisure journals and keep up to speed with the latest issues and topics of debate.

99

On a regular basis, review your CV and keep it up to date. Also keep a portfolio of evidence of the activities with which you have been involved. Under pressure to meet the closing date for a job application, it is surprising how difficult it is to lay your hands on the information that you require. Ensure that you write an application specific to the job description, not merely a standard response that you send out whatever the nature of the post advertised.

100

If you are selected for interview, show your genuine enthusiasm for sports development. Demonstrate that you are self-motivated and have good communication skills and show how any previous experience and qualifications can be an asset to your potential new employer.

101

If sport is your interest and you like working with people, if you are self-motivated, prepared to work unsociable hours and enjoy a challenge, securing a post in sports development is well worth the effort. It may not make your fortune but it is a vocation you will be proud to be part of.

I wish you every success in achieving your career goals!

Appendix A

The Active Sports Programme

Sport England's suite of 'Active' Programmes form a crucial part of their 'More People' strategy which aims to involve more people, particularly young people, in more sport over the next five years. The three main elements are Active Sports, Active Schools and Active Communities and together they provide a comprehensive sports development system that is co-ordinated nationally but delivered locally. The cornerstone of their development strategy is to encourage a partnership approach, bringing together all relevant organisations to provide services and resources to meet identified local needs. The Active Programmes dovetail into the World Class programmes, providing a comprehensive sports performance pathway. This can be linked into the Sports Development Continuum/Sports Performance Pathway (Appendix B) to provide a model of the 'bigger picture' for sports development in England.

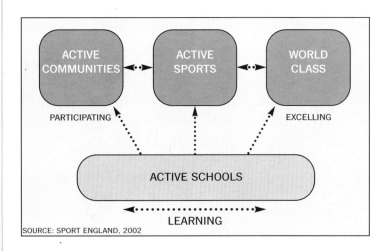

SOURCE: SPORT ENGLAND, 2002

Appendix B

The Sports Development Continuum/ Sports Performance Pathway

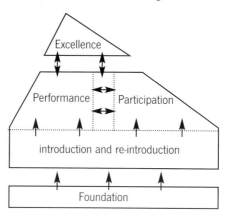

The figure above is a common representation of the Sports Development Continuum that indicates the flow between the levels of foundation, participation, performance and excellence. This representation suggests that there is a conscious decision made by the individual when moving to and from participation and performance, and performance and excellence levels. Recognised within the context of this framework are the principles of sports equity, the need for sustainability and the recognition that many organisations, agencies and individuals have a valuable contribution to make to the overall process.

More recently, the above continuum has been repackaged as the 'Sports Performance Pathway' which replaces foundation with 'getting started', participation with 'getting involved', performance with 'getting better' and excellence with 'being the best'.

Whatever the terminology, the model is a tool to help identify the needs and the resources required as a part of your sports development planning process. This can be linked into the Active Programmes (Appendix A) to provide a model of the 'Bigger Picture' for sports development in England.

Appendix C

Bibliography

BOOKS

The books listed here can be viewed at ILAM's Information Centre but are only available for loan. In addition to this, the Information Centre can provide reading lists on sports related topics from its database containing reference books, reports and journal articles. Please contact the ILAM Information Centre for further details on tel: 01491 874841 or email infocentre@ilam.co.uk

0020643   604.03 LAW
CENTRAL COUNCIL FOR PHYSICAL RECREATION
A partnership for sport.
CENTRAL COUNCIL FOR PHYSCIAL RECREATION 2000
This document has been produced by the following governing bodies Amateur Swimming Association, The England & Wales Cricket Board, The Football Association, The Lawn Tennis Association, The Rugby Football League, Rugby Football Union and UK Athletics and came together to put sport's case to Government. 14pp

0019603   604.014 COA
COALTER, FRED; ALLISON, MARY; TAYLOR, JOHN;
Role of sport in regenerating deprived urban areas.
SCOTTISH EXECUTIVE CENTRAL RESEARCH UNIT 2000
In depth research report with ten case studies on urban regeneration in deprived areas and the role of sport. includes sections on sport and health, sport and crime, sport, young people and education, sport and employment, community development and volunteers, sport and ethnic minorities, and the environmental value of sport. 113pp

0020685   604.03 DEP
DEPARTMENT FOR CULTURE, MEDIA AND SPORT
A sporting future for all: the government's plan for sport.
DEPARTMENT FOR CULTURE, MEDIA AND SPORT 2001
A sporting future for all set out the government's vision for sport and its potential

as a powerful tool for social, educational and physical well-being. A sport strategy implementation group was set up to identify what needed to be done to bring the strategy to life and produced an action plan for putting recommendations in practice. 44pp

0020604   600.155 ENG
ENGLISH FEDERATION OF DISABILITY SPORT
A four year sports development plan for disabled people in England 2000 - 2004.
SPORT ENGLAND 2000
A plan setting out a four-year strategic framework in which the work priorities for the EFDS are identified from April 2000 to March 2004. The plan provides background information about the EFDS as a new umbrella organisation for disability sport in England, comprising 7 National Disability Sports Organisations and 10 Regional Federations. 76pp.

0019085   604.5 QUE
QUEST
QUEST for sports development: manager's guidance pack.
QUEST 2000
Quality scheme framework for sports development managers. Includes introduction to QUEST, criteria for quality in sports development, self-assessment and planning guidance, and information on external assessment. Loose-leaf binder with loose sheets for self assessment. 101pp

0022860   604.522 SPO
SPORT ENGLAND
Performance measurement for the development of sport - a good practice guide for local authorities
SPORT ENGLAND 2001
This publication is part of a Tool Kit of information, guidance and services that Sport England is developing to assist local authorities to deliver Best Value through sport. The full version of this guidance is available on the Sport England website: www.sportengland.org

0018983   604.01 SPO
SPORT ENGLAND
Planning across boundaries: guidance on local strategies for the development of sport.
SPORT ENGLAND 1999
Part of the Best Value through sport toolkit developed to help local authorities

deliver best value strategies through sport. Includes national and regional context, and local strategies. 72pp.

0018982   604.01 SPO
SPORT ENGLAND
Planning for sport: ten key steps to producing a sports development plan.
SPORT ENGLAND   1999
One of the Running Sport series produced by Sport England. This workbook is a resource pack for a planning sport workshop which enables users to describe, outline and plan the sports development process.

0020550   604.08 SPO
SPORT ENGLAND
Running sport: the business of sports development.
NATIONAL COACHING FOUNDATION 2000
Running sport is the education and training programme of Sport England, covering a wide range of topics in the area of sports management and sports development.

0017311   600.19 SPO
The value of sport
SPORT ENGLAND 1999
Policy document considering the value of sport to society. Uses scientific evidence and examples of good practice to demonstrate that sport can make a difference to the quality of life of individuals and communities. Covers: definitions; international importance; social value; participation; volunteers; health; education; communities; economy and environmental issues. 40pp.

0020569   600.163 ENG
SPORTS COUNCIL
Sportslink
SPORTS COUNCIL 1999
Creating and developing school/club links. This is an introductory booklet in the Sports Council Running Sport programme. 12pp

0022094   600.162 SPO
SPORT ENGLAND
Keeping children safe in sport
NATIONAL SOCIETY FOR THE PREVENTION OF CRUELTY TO CHILDREN 2001
'Keeping Children Safe in Sport' has been designed to help sports organisations

deal appropriately with child protection issues. It will help clubs safeguard the children in their care by enabling staff and volunteers to recognise and understand their role in child protection. This leaflet sets out the benefits.

0024545   130.45 VOL
VOLUNTEER INVESTMENT PROGRAMME
Volunteer Investment Programme Welcome Pack

SPORT ENGLAND 2002
Introductory pack for the Volunteer Investment programme. Includes Volunteering Matters a 16 page guide, a factsheet on the national minimum wage act, and guidance on the 1997 good practice awards.

0022431   600.15121 WOM
WOMENS SPORTS FOUNDATION & SPORT ENGLAND
National action plan for women's and girls' sport and physical activity
SPORT ENGLAND 2000
The action plan aims to create a positive environment in which all women and girls have an equal opportunity and adequate resources to be involved in all areas of physical activity and sport, in an activity of their choice at their chosen level and capacity. 14pp

BOOKS AVAILABLE TO PURCHASE FROM THE ILAM BOOKSHOP

These books are available to purchase from ILAM. The ILAM Bookshop can also supply a complete list of sport titles. Please contact the Bookshop for further information on tel: 01491 874842

0020440
HYLTON, K.; BRAMHAM, P.; ET AL
Sports development: policy, process and practice
ROUTLEDGE 2001
Considers all aspects of good practice in sports development exploring every level of policy and practice. Includes: resources; sport for all; community sports development; partnerships; health; legal principles.

0025393
HOULIHAN, B.; WHITE, A.
The politics of sports development: Development of sport, or development through sport?
ROUTLEDGE 2002
This text explores the origins and evolution of sports development from the early years of public policy for sport to the present day, and sets this against a background of policy initiatives and an examination of contemporary political emphasis on sport as a part of social and cultural well-being.

0023893
ELLISON, E.
101 Ways to implement the disability discrimination act (DDA)
ILAM 2002
This book is aimed at people and organisations within the leisure industry that provides a service, offer facilities or supply goods to the public. It focuses on the Disability Discrimination Act (DDA) which seeks to end discrimination against disabled people. The rights that disabled people now have under the Act are explained and the service provider's duty to comply with all section of the act is clarified.

0020455
ILAM BEST VALUE WORKING GROUP
101 Ways to approach a best value review
ILAM 2001
Designed as a simple guide to undertaking a best value review from the initial scoping through to inspection. Specific attention is given to community needs and demands, strategic aims and objectives of an authority and the government's agenda. Offers a logical approach to the four Cs of best value.

0020106
BONE, V.; MITCHELL, E.
101 Ways to develop a local cultural strategy
ILAM 2000
Gives pragmatic and practical guidance on how to make best use of the process of developing a local cultural strategy for those leading or actively involved in steering groups. A series of case studies from a range of local authorities illustrates key points.

JOURNAL ARTICLES

0020203
CAMPBELL, SUE
Indentifying these vital questions of sport.
RECREATION (2000 November; p19-21)
Review of sports education and sports development by the Government's special adviser on sport. Looks at sport and culture, quality, club development and social exclusion.

0019863
CHAUDHARY, VIVEK
Girls given sporting chance.
GUARDIAN (2000 10 November; p10)
Researchers for the Girls in Sport campaign, launched by Nike and the Youth Sports Trust, have found from a two year pilot survey that girls in secondary level education tend to drop out of sport because they object to competitive games, communal changing and out of date PE kit. Where changes to non-competitive games were introduced, together with changes in kit and facilities, drop out rates were almost halved.

0024027
EVANS, DAVID
The big issue
LOCAL GOVERNMENT NEWS (2002 February; p93)
Report on the issues facing sport in the UK from the ILAM president, David Evans. Includes government strategies. Those of regional sports boards, local sports funding and development of specialist sports colleges and school sports co-ordinator programmes.

0022581
GARDNER, T.; SMYTH, I.; ALLEN, C.; & MCQUADE, S.
The National Occupational Standards: Coaching Skills
FASTER, HIGHER, STRONGER (2001 October; Issue 13; p10-15)
This information brochure includes - planning coaching sessions; dealing with accidents and emergencies; relationships between the coach and the performer; and the coach: the doctor of sport?

0025176
GOLD, KAREN
Fun comes first
SUNDAY TIMES EDUCATION (2002 16 June; p10)

Sport England has produced a sports day toolkit which will be piloted by 100 primary schools this summer. The schools will set up zones on their sports field, moving teams children between them to score points in different activities which will test skill, understanding and ability as well as speed. The system permits all children to be involved, and offers opportunities for less athletic pupils to succeed. Information on the tool-kit is available at www.sportengland.org/active_schools

0022390
HENDLEY, K.
School sports co-ordinators: one year old.
SPORTSTEACHER (2001 Autumn; p51-53)
Considered by some to be the most exciting development in school sport for years, and by others as a role fraught with hidden pitfalls, School Sports Co-ordinators are now one year old. This article considers progress so far and looks at how the programme is working in Nottinghamshire.

0019499
ILAM launches "First" service for sports officers
LEISURE NEWS & JOBS (2000 21-27 September; p2)
First is an electronic newsletter containing news and information on Sports Development and which is made available to Sports Development Officers. Email first@ilam.co.uk for details.

0017359
STEWART, D.
Safety in sport
SPORT AND THE LAW JOURNAL (1998 6(1); p41-46)
Considers the issue of liability in amateur sport, with views on the status of volunteer officials and coaches in the case of accidents

0024133
WINT, S. de.
Employment of coaches in youth sport development.
SPORT AND THE LAW JOURNAL (2001 Vol 9; Issue 3; p174-180)
For years many people have claimed that sport in the United Kingdom (UK), and England in particular has been underpinned by a massive voluntary sector. In 1995 it was estimated that the total annual value of the UK sports volunteer market was over £1.5 billion. Since this period however there have been some remarkable changes in how sport is run within the UK. 6p

ILAM FACT SHEETS

0023439
Fact Sheet 01/8: Funding sources for sport
INSTITUTE OF LEISURE AND AMENITY MANAGEMENT 2001
Information on funding sources for sport, with contact details and websites. 4pp

0023437
Fact Sheet 01/6: Information sources on the internet:
INSTITUTE OF LEISURE AND AMENITY MANAGEMENT 2001
Listing of useful sources for information on arts, environment, sport, government, play, tourism and statistics. 4pp

0020377
EDWARDS, MARIA
Fact Sheet 01/2: Lottery funding: contacts and resources
INSTITUTE OF LEISURE AND AMENITY MANAGEMENT 2001
Brief listing of websites and phone numbers of organisations associated with administration of the lottery funding to leisure, sports, the arts and other lottery recipients. 2pp

0020068
Fact Sheet 00/7: Free-standing goal frames
INSTITUTE OF LEISURE AND AMENITY MANAGEMENT 2000
Information on the issues surrounding the use of portable goal frames. Replaces Fact Sheet 96/8: Free standing goal frames, safety considerations. 2pp

0018177
Fact Sheet 98/7: Child protection in sport
INSTITUTE OF LEISURE AND AMENITY MANAGEMENT 1998
Detailed briefing note on protecting children from abuse. Defines types of abuse, provides details of Home Office guidance, and lists basic procedures for policy and procedure, recruitment, and education and training. Includes bibliography of further reading and list of contacts. 4pp

0012376
Fact Sheet 97/5: Disability Discrimination Act: Issues and guidelines
INSTITUTE OF LEISURE AND AMENITY MANAGEMENT 1997
Basic guidance on the provisions of the Act. 2pp

WEBSITES

British Sports Trust
Information about the various national recognised Sport Leader Awards and how to get involved
http://www.bst.org.uk

Central Council for Physical Recreation
Information about the organisation, government initiatives and funding, tax relief for sports clubs.
http://www.ccpr.org.uk

Department for Culture Media and Sport
Information about the department and its work, including a what's new page and other links and publications.
http://www.culture.gov.uk

English Federation of Disability Sport
Organisation promoting disability sport.
http://www.efds.co.uk

English Institute of Sport
Information on sport in the UK, case studies on sport, and the development of the EIS network.
http://www.eis2win.co.uk

Football Foundation
Partnership initiative delivering investment to grassroots football.
http://www.footballfoundation.org.uk

National Council for School Sport
National forum body for school sports associations.
http://www.schoolsport.freeserve.co.uk

Physical Education Association
Promotes, develops and sustains high quality physical education in the UK.
http://www.pea.uk.com

Sport and Recreation Industry Training Organisation
Provides organisational information, activities and

publications. Information included on S/NVQs, Investors in People, graduate recruitment and other training opportunities.
http://www.sprito-els.org.uk

Sport England
Information about Sport England's work, including information on the Lottery Sports Fund and the UK Sports Institute.
http://www.sportengland.org

Sport Scotland (Scottish Sports Council)
Sport Scotland is the national agency dedicated to promoting sporting opportunities for all Scots at all levels, whatever their interest and ability. Sport 21, Scotland's national strategy for sport. is led by Sport Scotland.
http://www.sportscotland.org.uk

Sporting Equals
Promoting racial equality within sport
http://cre.gov.uk/speqs

Sports Coach UK
Previously the National Coaching Foundation. Details of products, courses and information resources. Also has links to related sites.
http://www.sportscoachuk.org

Sports Council for Wales
Information on the sports strategies for Wales, including Best Value, and the services available from the Sports Council for Wales.
http://www.sports-council-wales.co.uk/

Sports Council Northern Ireland
Information on the strategy for developing sport in Northern Ireland 1997-2005, with contacts and links
http://www.sportni.org/

Sports Industry Federation

Federation of trade associations in the sports sector. Includes information on membership benefits and existing members organisations.

http://www.sportsdata.co.uk

Sports On Line

Useful information on sports clubs and sports participation and includes listings of further and higher education establishments and their leisure related courses.

http://www.sportsonline.co.uk

UK Sport (UK Sports Council)

The site provides an overview of sport in the UK and a detailed look at what UK Sport is doing to help UK athletes. Includes search options and links to key UK and International sporting organisations.

http://www.uksport.gov.uk

Wired for Health

A joint initiative between the DfES and DoH for promoting health to young people. Includes guidance on health initiatives for sports teachers and coaches.

http://www.wiredforhealth.gov.uk

Women's Sports Foundation

Promoting sport for women and equal opportunities within sport.

http://www.wsf.org.uk

Youth Sport Trust

Online source of information for those working in sport with young people.

http://www.youthsport.net